Feb 19

LIFE WITH
CYSTIC FIBROSIS

BY JEANNE MARIE FORD

Published by The Child's World®
1980 Lookout Drive • Mankato, MN 56003-1705
800-599-READ • www.childsworld.com

Content Consultant: Nauman Chaudary, M.D., Associate Professor of Medicine,
Virginia Commonwealth University

Photographs ©: SPL/Science Source, cover, 1; Shutterstock Images, 5, 10; Patrick
Reddy/The Cincinnati Enquirer/AP Images, 6; iStockphoto, 9, 18; AdMedia/Splash
News/Newscom, 12; Narin Phapnam/Shutterstock Images, 15; Monkey Business
Images/Shutterstock Images, 16; BSIP/Newscom, 20

ISBN 9781503825093
LCCN 2017959678

Printed in the United States of America
PA02375

TABLE OF CONTENTS

FAST FACTS

- Cystic fibrosis (CF) runs in families. It is caused by a **gene** that is **inherited** from both parents.

- If both parents have the CF gene, each of their children has a one-in-four chance of inheriting the disease. People with the CF gene who don't have the disease are called carriers.

- In CF, thick mucus builds up in the lungs. The mucus causes trouble with breathing. People with CF may have a persistent cough. Mucus also builds up around the pancreas. The pancreas produces **enzymes**. Enzymes aid digestion in the intestines. But the mucus keeps enzymes from reaching the intestines. Because of their digestive problems, people with CF have difficulty gaining weight.

- There is no cure for CF. Daily breathing treatments help clear the airways. Enzyme pills make it easier to digest food.

- More than 70,000 people worldwide live with CF.

- The average life expectancy of a person with CF is 47 years. But some people live much longer. New drugs are being developed that target the cause of the disease. They may increase the lifespan of some CF patients by many years.

CF AND THE LUNGS

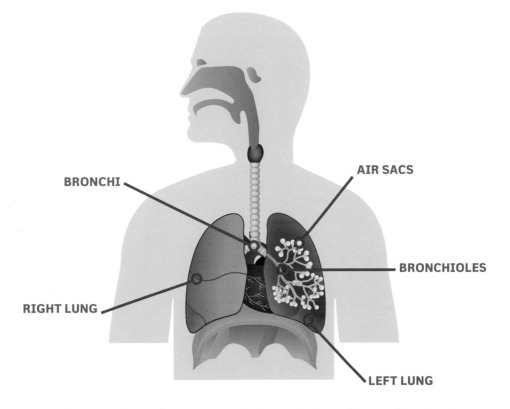

When you breathe, air travels through breathing tubes in the lungs called bronchi (BRONGK-eye), then into smaller tubes called bronchioles (BRONGK-ee-ohls). At the end of the bronchioles are air sacs. Oxygen passes into blood vessels that surround the air sacs. The blood vessels transport the oxygen throughout the body. Cells in the bronchi produce thin mucus. The mucus traps germs so you can cough them up. But the CF gene causes this mucus to be thick.

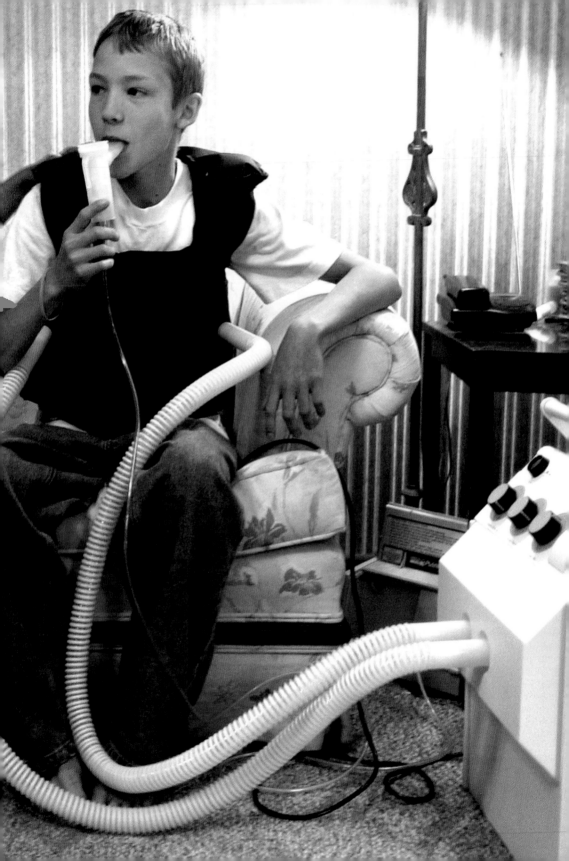

Chapter 1

CONNOR'S TREATMENT

The black vest squeezed ten-year-old Connor's chest like a blood pressure cuff. When it jiggled, his whole body shook. His mom pressed the button to turn on his **nebulizer**. He breathed in liquid medicine droplets from the nebulizer.

Connor's nebulizer treated his cystic fibrosis. The vest helped loosen the thick mucus in his lungs so he could cough it out more easily. The nebulizer delivered small droplets of medicines into his lungs. Connor did two breathing treatments each day. When he had a lung infection, he did four.

◄ **Daily breathing treatments help people with CF cough up the mucus in their lungs.**

Connor's younger brother, William, plopped down on a chair across the room. William had cystic fibrosis, too. He was wearing his own vest and had his own nebulizer. CF made both Connor and William prone to infections.

To avoid spreading germs to each other, they needed stay at least 6 feet (2 m) apart. They also couldn't share nebulizer machines, toys, or other items.

William had a video game controller in his hand. He asked Connor which video game he wanted to play. Connor grabbed a controller, and they turned on the video game.

INFECTIONS

An infection is a disease or illness caused by the spread of germs. Infections are common in people with CF. The thick mucus in their lungs traps **bacteria** that cause infections. The mucus also feeds the bacteria and helps them grow. Doctors use **antibiotics** to fight these infections. Frequent infections can cause permanent damage to the lungs of CF patients.

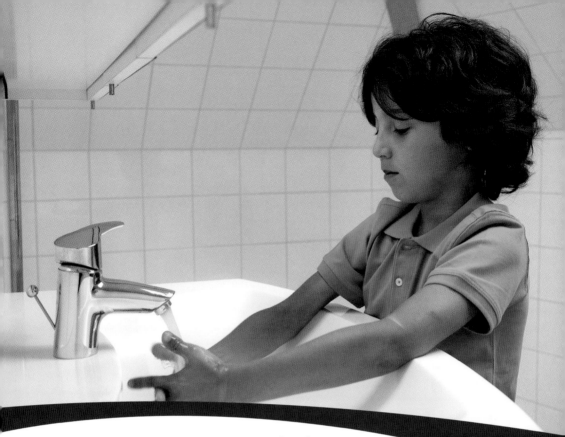

▲ People with CF wash their hands often to avoid infections.

The two nebulizers hummed loudly. Connor turned up the volume on the television so he could hear the music. He coughed. The treatment made it feel as though someone was pounding on his chest. He was used to it, but sometimes it hurt. The game and his brother's company were good distractions.

Connor's nebulizer treatment was a part of his morning routine just as much as brushing his teeth.

▲ High-calorie protein powder, which can be added to milk, can help people with CF gain weight.

So were the six enzyme pills Connor took each day with breakfast to help him digest his food. His mom stirred a high-**calorie** powder into his chocolate milk each day. The extra calories helped him gain weight.

At school, Connor was careful to try to avoid germs. He did not share any school supplies with his classmates. He washed his hands often. He knew a simple cold could turn into a serious illness. He'd been hospitalized twice this year already.

Many of Connor's friends played on sports teams after school. He wished he could join them. Instead, he had to go straight home to have a treatment.

When Connor's nebulizer treatment was finished, he felt great. He soaked his nebulizer in an **antibacterial** solution. This would get rid of germs so that he would have clean equipment for his next breathing treatment.

Connor went outside with his brother to play soccer. William kicked the ball to him. Connor kicked the ball into the net and made a goal. Playing with his brother was his favorite part of the day. He couldn't wait to do it again tomorrow.

Chapter 2

TRAVIS FLORES

A deep, curving scar cut across the middle of Travis Flores's chest. He wore it proudly. Without his scar, he knew he would not be alive.

Travis had been diagnosed with CF when he was just four months old. He was eight years old when he was hospitalized for the first time. At first, he was excited to have a break from school. Then he realized how sick some of the other kids with CF were. He decided to write a book to encourage them to keep fighting. The book was published in 2004, when Travis was 13 years old. Travis donated the book's profits to charities that helped kids with CF and other serious illnesses.

◄ Travis Flores (left) attends a movie premiere in 2016 with friend and activist Shira Strongin (right).

THE CYSTIC FIBROSIS FOUNDATION

The Cystic Fibrosis Foundation raises money to find new treatments for CF. In 1965, volunteer Mary G. Weiss had three young sons with CF. Her four-year-old, Richard, misheard the words "cystic fibrosis." He thought his mom was saying "65 roses." The CF Foundation began to use the phrase "65 roses" to make more people aware of the disease. The rose is now the group's symbol. It stands for love and hope for a cure.

Travis knew he had no time to waste in his life. He went to college when he was 16 years old and graduated when he was 20. He earned a master's degree and became a professional fund-raiser. He raised more than $1 million for the Cystic Fibrosis Foundation.

As Travis entered his early twenties, his lung infections became harder to treat. He needed an oxygen tank to help him breathe.

Oxygen tanks can store and deliver oxygen to people who ▶ have difficulty breathing.

It took a huge effort to say a single sentence. Travis couldn't walk from his bed to the bathroom. He was afraid to go to sleep because he thought he might not wake up.

Doctors said Travis probably wouldn't live much longer unless he tried a new treatment. They gave him a double lung **transplant** from an organ donor. With new lungs after his transplant surgery, Travis could finally take a deep breath. He could do things he'd never done before, such as biking on the beach or hiking a steep canyon.

Travis had healthy lungs now, but he still had CF. He still had to take dozens of pills each day. These included medications to prevent his body from rejecting his new lungs. Although he was not cured, he had a chance to live a full life again.

◄ **With proper treatment, people with CF may be able to enjoy many activities, such as hiking.**

Chapter 3

SABRINA WALKER

abrina Walker settled her son in a jogging stroller. Then she took off down the icy sidewalks of her neighborhood in Anchorage, Alaska. At first, the sound of her breathing filled her ears. She coughed and wheezed loudly. But after a while, her lungs began to clear.

Sabrina was four years old when she was diagnosed with CF. At the time, kids with CF were not expected to live nearly as long as they are today. She was told she probably wouldn't make it past the age of eight. When she was younger, there was no special vest to break up the mucus in her lungs. Instead, her parents thumped on her chest from different angles to help it drain out.

◀ **Exercise, including running, can help loosen mucus in the lungs so people with CF can more easily cough it up.**

▲ Physical therapists can show people with CF exercises that help clear out their airways.

Sabrina began running when she was 12 years old. She started by trying to jog for ten minutes at a time. By the time she reached high school, she had become a member of her school's cross-country team.

After she graduated from high school, Sabrina was diagnosed with cancer. Her CF made it harder for doctors to treat her cancer. But Sabrina was tough, and she endured the treatments. The cancer went away. She got married. She later got pregnant and had a baby.

Her husband had a low chance of being a CF carrier, and her baby was born without CF.

After her baby was born, Sabrina was hospitalized for a lung infection and pneumonia, a disease that affected her ability to breathe. When she was released, she carried antibiotics in a backpack. A tube delivered the medicine into a vein in her arm. She strapped on the backpack and went right back to running.

Sabrina now races competitively several times each year. She believes there will be a cure for CF in her lifetime. In the meantime, she continues to run and stay active.

THINK ABOUT IT

- Think of your favorite sport or activity. How might you adapt it for someone who has CF?
- If you had CF, do you think it would be easier or harder to have a sibling who also had the disease?
- Would you want to know if you were a carrier of CF?

GLOSSARY

antibacterial (an-ti-bak-TEER-ee-uhl): Something that is antibacterial fights against bacteria. An antibacterial solution can help people with cystic fibrosis keep their equipment clean.

antibiotics (an-ti-bye-OT-ikz): Antibiotics are medicines that treat infections caused by bacteria. Many people with cystic fibrosis take antibiotics every day.

bacteria (bak-TEER-ee-uh): Bacteria are germs that cause infection. Certain bacteria are very dangerous to people with cystic fibrosis.

calorie (KAL-uh-ree): A calorie is a unit used to measure the amount of energy in food. Because people with cystic fibrosis have trouble with digestion, high-calorie foods help them get the extra nutrients they need.

enzymes (EN-zymez): Enzymes are proteins produced by the body that have many functions, including aiding in digestion. In people with cystic fibrosis, mucus blocks enzymes from reaching the intestines.

gene (JEEN): A gene is located within the body's cells and determines which traits are inherited from parents. A gene for cystic fibrosis causes the disease under certain conditions.

inherited (in-HAIR-it-id): A trait is inherited when it is passed down by parents to their children. Cystic fibrosis is caused by a gene that is inherited from both parents.

nebulizer (NEHB-yoo-lyz-er): A nebulizer is a machine that delivers inhaled medication. Cystic fibrosis patients typically use a nebulizer twice each day.

transplant (TRANS-plant): A transplant is an operation that replaces a diseased organ with a healthy one. A lung transplant can extend the life of a person with severe cystic fibrosis.

TO LEARN MORE

Books

Bjorklund, Ruth. *Cystic Fibrosis*. New York, NY: Marshall Cavendish, 2009.

Glynne, Andy, Nandita Jain, and Salvador Maldonado. *Jasper's Story: Living with Cystic Fibrosis*. London, UK: Franklin Watts, 2017.

Gray, Susan H. *The Respiratory System*. Mankato, MN: The Child's World, 2015.

Web Sites

Visit our Web site for links about cystic fibrosis:

childsworld.com/links

Note to Parents, Teachers, and Librarians: We routinely verify our Web links to make sure they are safe and active sites. So encourage your readers to check them out!

SELECTED BIBLIOGRAPHY

"About Cystic Fibrosis." *Cystic Fibrosis Foundation*. Cystic Fibrosis Foundation, n.d. Web. 4 Dec. 2017.

Lester, Marc. "The Run of a Lifetime." *Anchorage Daily News*. Alaska Dispatch Publishing, 13 Mar. 2016. Web. 4 Dec. 2017.

Orenstein, David M., David Weiner, and Jonathan Spahr. *Cystic Fibrosis: A Guide for Patient and Family*. Wolters Kluwer Health, 2015.

INDEX

ABOUT THE AUTHOR

Jeanne Marie Ford is an Emmy-winning TV scriptwriter who holds an MFA in Writing for Children from Vermont College. She has written numerous children's books and articles and also teaches college English. She lives in Maryland with her husband and two children.